P9-DGC-064

PRESENTED TO

FROM

DATE

THE

Great

STEVEN CURTIS CHAPMAN

Adventure

J. COUNTRYMAN

NASHVILLE, TENNESSEE

Each of us, regardless of where we are in the journey of life, are constantly moving somewhere, whether drifting off the path or moving ahead with our eyes firmly set on the final prize. Yet our journey, the adventure of life, is more than simply moving toward a destination, it's a mindset about the journey itself.

I discovered this in a profoundly new way just prior to recording *The Great Adventure.* At that time, as a father, husband, follower of Christ, recording artist—basically in every area of life, I felt somewhat like a failure. It was a very discouraging time for me. My wife, Mary Beth, and I had been at odds, and it seemed that I wasn't communicating with my kids or being as good a dad as I wanted to be.

I was feeling pretty low when I met with my pastoral advisory board to go over some new ideas for a yet-untitled album. After we had exchanged casual greetings and pleasantries, someone asked me how I was doing. Half-jokingly, I replied, "Well, I really feel like I just need to sit and cry for a while." Then I laughed and said, "It's just been a hard week."

One of the pastors understood that something was bothering me far more than I was admitting. He said, "I want to go back to something you said earlier. You said something about feeling you just needed to sit and cry. Why did you say that?"

His question was an invitation for the floodgates to open, and the tears started to flow down my face. I told them how I felt like I was a miserable husband and that my devotional time with God felt empty. Everything in my life, it seemed, was either crashing down or teetering on the edge. "I just don't feel like I'm doing very well," I admitted.

Then these guys began to encourage me and lift me up. As I shared my heartaches with them, they shared a concept with me that totally blew me away. It was a moment of epiphany that changed the way I looked at life from then on.

The concept is this: because of God's grace, there is nothing we can do that will make Him love us more than He already does. And there is nothing we can do or have done that will cause Him to love us any less. Our performance in life doesn't affect His acceptance of us, or His love for us. Now that doesn't give us a license for unacceptable behavior, but it does release us from the bondage of our failures.

This was such an amazing and refreshing concept to me. It was as if the four walls surrounding me had come crashing down. In fact, in the music video for "The Great Adventure," we actually filmed a sequence where I was trying to perform in a little tiny room and suddenly, the walls fall away and the huge, grand landscape of God's grace opens up to me.

I realized that was where I had been standing all along. I had been bound within the confines of the little box only by my limited understanding. Once those walls were knocked down, I was out in the wide-open spaces of God's grace.

Eugene Peterson says it this way in his translation of Romans 5 in *The Message*: "We throw open our doors to God and discover at the same moment that he has already thrown open his door to us. We find ourselves standing where we always hoped we might stand—out in wide open spaces of God's grace and glory, standing tall and shouting our praise."

It's this incredible truth, and the revelation and experience of it in my own life that inspired not only the song and the album title, *The Great Adventure*, but also this book. Jesus explained in John 10 that He came so that we might have life and live it fully and completely for all it was created to be . . . a life of adventure. As with any adventure, there will surely be mountains to climb, valleys to trudge through, moments of breathtaking scenery from the peaks, and seasons of wondering where we are. We will experience sorrow that at times seems almost unbearable, as well as joy that's unspeakable. After all, this is life, but because of the grace of God we can experience it and live it to the fullest.

In the pages that follow, I've shared some of what I've learned about God's amazing grace in hopes that you, too, will experience life as the incredible adventure God created it to be. My prayer is that Jesus would bless you abundantly as you travel on the exciting journey He has planned for you.

STEVEN CURTIS CHAPMAN

THE GREAT ADVENTURE

Saddle up your horses
Started out this morning in the usual way
Chasing thoughts inside my head of all I had to do today
Another time around the circle try to make it better than the last
I opened up the Bible and I read about me
Said I'd been a prisoner and God's grace had set me free
And somewhere between the pages it hit me like a lightening bolt
I saw a big frontier in front of me and I heard somebody say let's go!

CHORUS:

Saddle up your horses we've got a trail to blaze
Through the wild blue yonder of God's amazing grace
Let's follow our leader into the glorious unknown
This is a life like no other oh . . . this is The Great Adventure! Yeah . . .

Come on get ready for the ride of your life
Gonna leave long faced religion in a cloud of dust behind
And discover all the new horizons just waiting to be explored
This is what we were created for

CHORUS

Bridge:
We'll travel over, over mountains so high
We'll go through valleys below
Still through it all we'll find that
This is the greatest journey that the human heart will ever see
The love of God will take us far beyond our wildest dreams
Yeah . . . oh saddle up your horses . . . come on get ready to ride

CHORUS

Courage

Be strong and of good courage,

do not fear nor be afraid of them: for the Lord

your God, He is the One who goes with you.

He will not leave you nor forsake you.

DEUTERONOMY 31:6

What do you think of when you hear the word *courage*? I picture a scene where soldiers armed with shields and swords are running into battle. They appear to have a boldness that makes them unafraid of anything! But much of their boldness is based on the strength of their sword and armor and physical skill. As Christian "soldiers," on the other hand, our boldness comes from the One who walks beside us and places His power within us.

As we journey on the adventure of life, God leads us. He walks ahead of us. He's the point man out there blazing the trail for us. Even on the days when we face doubts and fear, we can take courage from our faith in Him. We can take that first step out of our comfort zone because we know that He has gone before us.

I think we can learn a great lesson about courage from the Lion in *The Wizard of Oz*. As you remember, he actually had courage inside himself all along; he just needed to be put in a situation that allowed the courage to come out, a situation where someone needed his help so badly he didn't have time to ponder it and hope for courage. He just acted spontaneously, and there it was—courage. The first step of courage isn't taken in the midst of a battle; it's taken when you're willing to walk onto the battlefield and face the unknown.

If there is one person in the Bible who exhibited boldness regularly, it was David. Killing lions, bears, and giants can't be done by the cowardly! But where did David's courage come from? As David replied to Saul in I Samuel 17:37, "The

LORD, who delivered me from the paw of the lion and from the paw of the bear, He will deliver me from the hand of this Philistine."

David believed in the power of God to be active in his life. That gave him the courage to respond with boldness. And we can have the same boldness and courage if we have the same faith that David had. In fact, you may find as you travel along your particular journey that God will give you opportunities—"bears" and "giants" so to speak—to demonstrate the courage that is inside you. When you know that Almighty God Himself is with you and has made His power available to you, how can you hold back your courage? Go ahead and let out a big roar!

I know there is no turning back

Once my feet have left the ledge

And in the rush I hear a voice

That's telling me it's time to

take the leap of faith

So here I go I'm diving in . . .

"DIVE"

From the Sparrow Records release *Speechless*

Gratitude

AND WHATEVER YOU DO IN WORD OR DEED,

DO ALL IN THE NAME OF THE LORD JESUS, GIVING THANKS

TO GOD THE FATHER THROUGH HIM.

COLOSSIANS 3:17

As we travel the journey of life, we are guaranteed disappointment and discouragement. But one of the quickest cures for the blues and blahs, one of the best ways to renew a sense of optimism, is to find something to be grateful for. When we practice gratitude day by day and keep a sense of being thankful, we find ourselves giving thanks in every circumstance, both pleasant and painful.

I've never forgotten what a friend told me years ago: Every morning, our first thought should be, *Father, thank you. For you've allowed the sun to come up another day and you've allowed me to see another day. Now what do you have in store for this day?*

In other words, approach the day with a "Good morning, Lord" as opposed to "Good Lord, it's morning!"

I'm working on a song for my new album about this very idea. The story behind the lyrics actually begins with my pastor. Recently he told about traveling through the Swiss Alps by train and being overwhelmed with the beauty and majesty surrounding him. He was so busy trying to take in all the sights, he almost got a crick in his neck looking out of the windows. At the same time, he glanced across the aisle and noticed a young boy with his nose practically glued to the screen of a Game Boy®. He was not the least bit concerned to be missing all the majesty around him.

When my family and I went to the Grand Canyon, we, too, were surrounded with the awesome majesty of God's creation. As I stood at the edge of the canyon, tears came to my eyes. I couldn't believe the glorious view. It was like nothing I had ever seen. It was like looking at a glorious three-dimensional painting and discovering it was real!

So with those two stories in mind, I wrote a song about playing a Game Boy while sitting on the edge of the Grand Canyon, which describes what happens to us when we become so preoccupied with the trivial in life that we lose sight of the glorious. The chorus goes like this:

> *Sometimes it seems I'm playing Game Boy*
> *Standing in the middle of the Grand Canyon*
> *I'm eating junk food sitting at a gourmet feast*
> *I'm splashing in a puddle when I could be swimming in the ocean*
> *What's wrong with me*
> *Wake up and see the glory*

Like the song says, we can wake up and see the glory or we can see the Game Boy. It all depends on our perspective. I don't want to pass through this great adventure of life and miss one glimpse of God's glory, goodness, and grace. It's all around us. We've just got to keep our eyes open.

Remember your chains

Remember the prison that once held you

Before the love of God broke through

Remember the place you were without grace

When you see where you are now

Remember your chains

And remember your chains are gone

"Remember Your Chains"

From the Sparrow Records release

Heaven in the Real World

Temptation

No temptation has overtaken you except such as is common to man; but God is faithful, who will not allow you to be tempted beyond what you are able, but with the temptation will also make the way of escape, that you may be able to bear it.

1 CORINTHIANS 10:13

As Christians on the great adventure of life, we try not only to attach ourselves to everything that is of Christ but to detach ourselves from everything that is not of Christ. When we acknowledge temptation and resist it, we make a conscious decision to detach ourselves from sin, and in doing that, we find we are attached more firmly to Christ.

There's an awesome story in the Bible that puts temptation in perspective for me. It's the story in Genesis 39 that tells how Potiphar's wife tried to seduce Joseph, Potiphar's servant. Joseph didn't merely have to say "no" to temptation once; he had to stand strong against this woman's aggressive, persistent temptation. There were hundreds of ways he could have justified giving in to the seduction of a carnal relationship with her. After all, she was in a position of power, and he was merely a servant. She was eager and willing. It would have been so easy; it would have made such sense from a worldly point of view just to give in. But Joseph literally ran away from the temptation, even knowing that her vindictive pride would make him pay dearly for humiliating her.

For most of us, temptation is more passive, just a matter of pleasure or expediency. But I still like to use Joseph's method of resisting those temptations— I run!

This Scripture reminds me of the story a radio DJ recounted to me shortly after "Run Away" was released. At that time, this song was a single on the radio, and I was doing a concert for the radio station. A few days later this DJ got a telephone call from a man who had been flirting with the idea of having an affair. He was in his car on his way to rendezvous with this woman when he heard the song on the radio:

Strolling past Temptation Avenue
You hear so many voices calling you
Maybe you'll step in and
take a quick look around
Try to walk through it,
And you're gonna fall down . . .
You've gotta run away . . .

"Run Away" is a be-bop, musically happy, engaging kind of song, not the kind of musical style that tends to lend itself to dramatic, emotional life changes. But when this man heard that song, it impacted him so much that he pulled his car over to the side of the road and, in tears, repented of the road he was literally traveling down. He turned his car around, went home, and confessed to his wife. He told her, "This is what has been going on, I don't know what it is going to cost me now, but I want to make it right. I want to run from this temptation." Because he resisted temptation, he was able to restore his relationship with his wife and reconcile his marriage.

God is faithful to give us the strength to resist, but we have to take the first step in the right direction. And believe you me, we had better be running!

Honesty

LYING LIPS ARE AN ABOMINATION

TO THE LORD, BUT THOSE WHO DEAL

TRUTHFULLY ARE HIS DELIGHT.

PROVERBS 12:22

Honesty is saying what we mean, and meaning what we say. It is refusing to deceive ourselves or others. It means we don't have to worry about having anything to hide. There's a great freedom that comes from being honest. That's why I think it's one of the most important aspects of the adventure of life.

God delights in people who are truthful, who are honest, particularly when it costs something. This is a simple but powerful concept.

My wife and I discovered this truth when our daughter Emily was just five weeks old. We left our apartment to run an errand one night, and when we returned an hour later, there were fire trucks all over the neighborhood. I said, "Look! Something's on fire over there," and it turned out to be our apartment! It was a terrifying experience that started a year-long process of trying to recover from our losses, of sifting through the ashes of all that happened that night.

When we met with our landlord's insurance company, we discovered that we weren't covered by insurance—not one dime. They wanted to know detailed events of what happened that night, and during the course of our conversation with them, my wife explained that she had put the baby-bottle sterilizer on the stove full of water and turned it on. But she couldn't remember having turned it off when we left.

As soon as she said that, my first impulse was to deny it. After all we really didn't know for sure what had happened. I kept thinking, *If only she hadn't admitted that, we might have gotten off scot-free* . . . especially after they determined that we were going to be liable for *all* the damages. It turned out to be a huge bill, and we were just a young family getting started at that time. Our only possessions were a Honda Civic and an empty bank account.

But throughout the next few months, we felt such peace because we had told the truth, even though it cost us dearly. We had been honest and had not tried to cover anything up, so we were completely free to turn to God and say, "Lord, we don't have the money to pay for this. We don't even begin to know where it will come from. Lord, we need you to provide for us."

It was an amazing experience. God touched us profoundly and took care of that situation. We worked through the process and got the bill reduced to a much smaller amount. Over a period of time, we were able to pay back all of the money. We learned a big lesson in faith that year, and we also learned that honesty and truthfulness must be a basic part of our great adventure.

When it's all said and done

Have you done what you said

When it's all said and done

Have you done what you

said you would do

"SAID AND DONE"

From the Sparrow Records release *First Hand*

Creativity

FOR WE ARE HIS WORKMANSHIP, CREATED IN

CHRIST JESUS FOR GOOD WORKS, WHICH

GOD PREPARED BEFOREHAND

THAT WE SHOULD WALK IN THEM.

EPHESIANS 2:10

My wife, Mary Beth, recently got involved in photography. She even set up a makeshift darkroom in the little washroom off of my studio. One night Mary Beth and a girlfriend of hers developed some pictures in there. When they were done, they were as excited as a couple of kids. Mary Beth ran downstairs saying, "Hey, come look at this, you've got to see this!" She brought me upstairs, took the pictures out, and stood back, so proud and excited to show me what she had done. Although my wife would say she's not very creative, having seen the excitement in her eyes that night made me realize just how much creativity is a vital part of each one of us.

God created each of us in His own image. And I truly believe that He expresses Himself through us by means of our own creativity. We become co-creators with Him. Because of my profession, I get to be creative in a more pronounced way than most folks. But even those people, like my sweet wife, who say "I'm not the creative type," can become co-creators, whether it's by taking photos or raking leaves in the backyard.

I get the greatest enjoyment out of watching my kids be creative. When Caleb was younger, he would sit at the table for hours, just drawing and humming to himself. There's a perpetually childish aspect to creativity. A willingness to see things from a new perspective and a delight in the smallest discovery. I've always seen that as the glory of the Creator being expressed, even through the youngest heart.

There's also a unique sense of wonder wrapped up in the creative process. And that's what makes it such an important part of the great adventure of life. Wonder not only makes the adventure more interesting, it can also lift our spirits when the road is rough or spark a renewed interest when we find ourselves on one of those long stretches of mundane, day-to-day living.

I hope you'll never become cynical and hardened and forget that life is an

adventure, filled with wonder and creativity. Just look around you, and you will see the awesome ways that God has revealed His creativity. Let that be an inspiration to spark your own sense of wonder and creativity.

I can see the fingerprints of God
When I look at you
I can see the fingerprints of God
And I know it's true
You're a masterpiece
That all creation quietly applauds
And you're covered with the fingerprints of God

"Fingerprints of God"

From the Sparrow Records release

Speechless

Change

Therefore, if anyone is in Christ, he is a new creation; old things have passed away; behold, all things have become new.

2 Corinthians 5:17

have a confession to make: I'm a creature of comfort. I like to know what to expect. I'm not a big fan of change unless I can be in complete control of it, which is seldom the case.

But there are always going to be changes in my life, and in your life. I guarantee it. God created and designed the world like that, but He also created us to cope with it. And many times, the very change we want to run from can bring the reminder that we are in Christ. We are new creations, and He is constantly creating new things around us or recreating the old things within us. That's all part of the joy of the journey.

God gave us the ability to handle the bumps and bruises of this journey as well as the smooth sailing. And He has promised no matter what each day brings, no matter how many twists and turns along he way, He will be there with us. But our first impulse is usually to run from change, to nestle back into the comfort of routine and the well worn. To resist change, however, means to miss new opportunities. Which reminds me of a little saying my friend Jack Miller often says: *Risk or rust.* There are great risks in any adventure, but the alternative is to rust, to stay in place and become hardened and dried out.

A good friend of mine once told me how he taught his son the lesson of

God's spontaneity and surprises. His little boy loved to swing in his backyard more than almost anything else. So one night when the boy was tucked in bed and just about to fall asleep, my friend scooped him up in his arms and without a word, carried him out to the swing. He set the little fellow down and gently began to push him. The boy was fully awake by this time and asked, "What are you doing, Daddy?"

The dad didn't say anything. Out there under the stars, in the sweet night air, he just kept pushing the little boy. After a while, my friend stopped the swing and took the boy back inside and tucked him in bed.

With bright eyes and the cutest little smile, his son looked up at him and asked again, "Daddy, why did you do that?"

The dad replied, "Because you like to swing so much."

What a beautiful way to help lay a foundation for his son, teaching him that God is our heavenly Father who also likes to surprise us and do for us the things we least expect.

I like that story. And if you stop and think about it, life wouldn't be much of an adventure if we knew exactly what would happen around the next bend in the road. So hang on tight and get set for the ride of your life!

As I look back on the road I've traveled

I see so many times He carried me through

And if there's one thing I've learned in my life

My Redeemer is faithful and true

"MY REDEEMER IS
FAITHFUL AND TRUE"

From the Sparrow Records release *First Hand*

Humility

ALL OF YOU BE SUBMISSIVE TO

ONE ANOTHER, AND BE CLOTHED WITH

HUMILITY, FOR "GOD RESISTS THE PROUD,

BUT GIVES GRACE TO THE HUMBLE."

1 PETER 5:5

I've been blessed and honored in my life to receive abundant accolades and awards for the work I've done, but I have mixed emotions about the recognition. After all, I didn't create these talents and abilities. God did.

It's sort of like the days when I was growing up. The guys in the neighborhood and I used to ramp-jump on our bikes and get them pretty beat up. So every few Christmases we'd get a new bike. Now imagine if a few days after Christmas, all six of us met down on the neighborhood corner, each riding a new bike. Then we held a conference and decided which of us had been given the best bike and handed that person an award.

What could that person say? "Well, it's really just a gift from my mom and dad, so I don't know if I should receive an award." You have to admit it would be an awkward situation.

But that same thing often happens to me because my profession takes place on a public platform. I'm rewarded for the gifts that God has given me. People congratulate me on the awards and the songs and the recordings, but all of this is simply a result of God's gifts. True, there is some craftsmanship involved, but the truth of the matter is, I'm just like the kid with the new bike standing up and saying, "Hey, look at this gift my Father gave me."

And if you think about it, God's gifts aren't limited to creative talents. Every breath, every moment of life we are given in this world is a testament to His bountiful gifts. We can't take pride in what isn't ours, and nothing we have is really ours.

I have to remind myself that only God knows the heart. That's why I pray every day that my heart would be humble, that I would be "clothed" in humility. Now I'm not talking about a good ole' southern-boy attitude of "aw shucks," but a genuine attitude of the heart—an inner attitude that is demonstrated externally.

It helps me to approach humility as a mindset, a conscious decision. I wouldn't get out of bed, take a shower, step out of the shower dripping wet, and then immediately walk out the door. Neither do I want to step out into the world without the "clothes" of humility—a mindset I put on intentionally, just like I put on a jacket.

The lyrics of "Miracle of Mercy" are a constant reminder that when I take a deep-down, honest look at my heart I find pride lurking there. That's why I continually need God to bring me back to that place of recognizing my need for Him, of being humble. If a light suddenly revealed the hidden parts of my heart—what I know to be the weakest parts of myself—I wouldn't be able to stand in front of people without God's grace. That's why I continually run to Him and say, "I need Your grace and Your mercy, so I humble myself before You again."

God gives grace to the humble, and we desperately need His grace for every step of the journey.

If the walls could speak of the times I've been weak

When everybody thought I was strong

Could I show my face if it weren't for the grace

Of the one who's known the truth all along

"MIRACLE OF MERCY"

From the Sparrow Records release *Heaven in the Real World*

Integrity

FOR OUR BOASTING IS THIS . . . THAT WE

CONDUCTED OURSELVES IN THE WORLD IN

SIMPLICITY AND GODLY SINCERITY, NOT WITH

FLESHY WISDOM BUT BY THE GRACE OF GOD,

AND MORE ABUNDANTLY TOWARD YOU.

2 CORINTHIANS 1:12

Integrity is who we are when no one is looking, when our masks are down. When the lights are off and we're not on stage . . . that's when people see our true character. When we're put in pressure situations that turn the heat up in our lives, then people see what we're really like inside, whether we're persons of integrity or not.

A few years ago I faced a major crossroads in my career. My music, I was told, had the potential to reach a much broader audience. But the deeply spiritual, particularly Christian ideas behind the lyrics of my songs were limiting my mass appeal. If I would consider modifying the message, my songs could reach more people.

It seemed a worthy goal: to reach as many people with the message as possible. And that is certainly what I wanted to do. But when I examine what my ultimate goal should be, I try to adhere to one principle: What will please and honor God? What will bring Him glory in this situation? When I make my decisions based on that principle, I act in integrity and maintain a clear conscience. In the process of trying to do this consistently, I've continued to be amazed at how many opportunities I've had to reach more people than I ever imagined.

I know I will have a clear conscience only to the extent that I live with integrity in the midst of all the expectations around me. Which reminds me of my favorite definition of a clear conscience: "It's *not* doing everything right so I can say I did nothing wrong, but doing everything as unto God with the desire to please Him in all situations and relationships."

In *The Call*, Os Guinness talks about living for the audience of One. In other words, dancing through life like nobody is watching except the Lord of the Dance. He is the only One who really matters; He's the One who is watching. When we live our lives to please Him we can "dance like nobody's looking." We can quit worrying about what everyone else is going to say or think about us. When we do that, we experience an extraordinary freedom in Him.

That's why I think of integrity as freedom from tyranny—the tyranny of living for the approval of others. When we keep our consciences clear before the God of all grace, we walk in integrity. And how do we accomplish that? Our ability to have integrity is rooted in Christ, who forgave our transgressions once and for all when He died on the cross. Now, through His living Word and the power of His Holy Spirit, we can be people of integrity.

If we want to make the journey of life as men and women of integrity, we must let the cool winds of God's love blow into every corner of our heart, cleaning out every inch of self and filling it with the light of true faith—cool winds on a clear conscious.

I want my life to show

The kind of love that comes and goes

With the heartbeat of heaven

Loving, joyful, peaceful, patient

Kind and good and full of faith

Self-controlled and gentle

Oh the heart of heaven beats this way.

"HEARTBEAT OF HEAVEN"

From the Sparrow Records release *Heaven in the Real World*

Faith

... Let us lay aside every weight, and the sin which so easily ensnares us, and let us run with endurance the race that is set before us, looking unto Jesus, the author and finisher of our faith, who for the joy that was set before Him, endured the cross, despising the shame, and has sat down at the right hand of the throne of God.

Hebrews 12:1-2

I've spent much of this past year exploring this idea of "faith." In fact, it's the central theme for my new album. I've discovered that the key to understanding faith is understanding what it is anchored in.

It is not based in our own wisdom or knowledge but in Christ. Our faith must be nestled in Him. As Phillip Yancy says, "Faith is reason gone courageous." We can't depend on what we understand or feel comfortable with. We must fix our eyes on Jesus and know that He is the goal, the leader, the One who goes before us on this great adventure. And He knows exactly what is ahead because He has already finished the race.

But what about the times when it's difficult to have faith, when it seems that God isn't there? What keeps us going in times of hardship? We can choose to sit down and give up, or we can follow our fearless Leader, the One who knows us better than we know ourselves. The One who knows the ultimate goal He has for us and has the power to see it come to pass. He is guiding us through this process, even if we can't always understand it.

Our entire family learned about faith firsthand through the process of adopting our daughter Shaohannah Hope. When our daughter Emily was thirteen years old, she suggested the idea of bringing another child into our home, one who wasn't our own flesh and blood. That was a very unique idea for us, especially when we first began talking about it. We realized it was something that would take 100 percent faith.

Emily had her heart and hopes firmly set on this adoption. And as she began to pray, her mom's heart and my heart began to be open to the idea. Emily would leave notes beside our table pleading with us to keep our hearts open and to at least consider this idea. Mary Beth and I began to pray about it and took tiny steps of faith in that direction.

Basically our attitude was, "This is probably something we're not going to do, but because Emily has so much faith, we need to take steps in this direction and be open to it."

One little step led to another. Eventually we realized this was something we wanted to do. Inside our hearts we were saying, "We believe God has placed this before us. We believe this is what our adventure is supposed to be. We're scared because we don't know what the future looks like, but we know this is the right thing to do."

Many nights Mary Beth and I would lay in bed and cry as we talked through all the fears and questions we had. She would ask, "Is this the right thing to do? Are we doing the right thing?" And all I could answer was, "Sweetheart, you know this is not a safe thing, it's not a comfortable thing, it's not easy or reasonable. But we feel it is the right thing, and God will lead us one step at a time if we walk in faith and seek to do His will."

From the very beginning we wanted the adoption to be a family event, knowing that it would affect all of us for the rest of our lives. So we took the entire family to China to see Shaohannah Hope's birth country and to visit the orphanage where she spent the first seven months of her life. We wanted to experience it, so we would all know and understand this part of our family history. It was going to be part of our story as well.

We went to Beijing, China, and had a few days to get to know the culture. We went to the Great Wall of China, we ate the food, and we went to Tianamen Square and the Forbidden City. We ended up in Changsha, China, at a little hotel. We sat in our hotel room and waited while they brought this little baby down the hallway. Outside the door we heard someone say, "She's here," and we walked out and met our daughter Shoahanna Hope. Then we became a family of six.

Up to that point, we were wondering, "What is

this going to be like? What will it feel like? When we hold her, will we panic? Are we going to feel like she is part of us?" The amazing thing was that when they put her in our arms, the love was immediate. I looked at my wife, and I knew at that moment she would, as with any of our other children, lay down her life for this child. This was our daughter.

We are still having an adventure of faith. Shoahanna Hope has nights when she cries out in her sleep, and Mary Beth will sit up with her for two or three hours. The orphanage and the experiences Shoahanna had there are still a part of her inner life.

This baby girl has impacted all our lives. None of my children will ever be the same. I've seen positive changes in them and watched them develop a new understanding of spiritual adoption. Now they know more fully what we mean when we say that God has adopted us into His family by sending His Son to die on the cross for us.

God made us for walking on water, for stepping out in faith like Peter did. But once we start factoring in reason, and understanding, and safety, and comfortable living, we miss so much of the adventure we're really called to live, which is a life of faith. So I'd like to challenge you to step out in faith on the great adventure of life.

The sun sinks low and here I go
Wrestling with questions that refuse an answer
This path of faith can be a place
So barren of what I understand
I can hear the voice of fear
Saying let me show you another way
So I cry out my Lord, Jesus
It's in Your love for me
I find all that I need

"I Am Found in You"

From the Sparrow Records release *Greatest Hits*

Great Expectations

Ask, and it will be given to you; seek, and you will find; knock, and it will be opened to you. For everyone who asks receives, and he who seeks finds, and to him who knocks it will be opened.

MATTHEW 7:7-8

Dreams and aspirations are gifts that God places in our hearts. He put the gift of music in my heart. I've always loved music, even as a kid. The first concert I attended was of Andre Crouch and the Disciples. I was simply overwhelmed, watching those talented people who were passionate about what they believed and using their God-given talents for Him. At that point, I quietly began to dream of being able to do that myself someday. I was too much of a realist to tell anyone, "Hey, that's what I'm going to do someday." But deep inside I kept the dream alive.

I listen to my son Will Franklin say to me now, "Dad, I'm trying to decide if I want to be an NFL quarterback or play for the Lakers, the St. Louis Cardinals, or the Braves. Or maybe I'll be a Christian recording artist like you."

My first thought is, *Boy, you go ahead and dream big because you're probably going to end up about the same height as your dad and you'll need all those big dreams.* I have to bite my tongue and resist the temptation to bring Will back to reality. While the chances may not seem great for some of those dreams to come true, I want him to keep dreaming all the same.

I was blessed that my dreams came true. There can be a danger, however, if we pursue our dreams to the extent that they become our idols. What we have to keep in focus is our ultimate goal. In 2 Corinthians 5:9, Paul encourages us to make it our goal to please God above all else. This doesn't mean we have to throw away our dreams. After all, God is the One who says for us to believe the unbelievable.

Like everything else in the great adventure of life, dreaming is a process, not a destination. In the Christian music business, many, many people come to town with the dream of becoming a recording artist, but it doesn't happen. Many become discouraged and angry with God. But we have to remember that God doesn't neglect or forget our dreams; He sometimes just redirects them.

God is faithful to finish what He started when He placed the dream in our hearts. We may not know what it will look like in the end, but we do know that it will be incredible. It will always be glorious with God.

We've been invited with the Son

And we've been invited to come and . . .

Believe the unbelievable

Receive the inconceivable

And see beyond my wildest imagination

Lord, I come with great expectations

"Great Expectations"

From the Sparrow Records release *Speechless*

Friendships

GREATER LOVE HAS NO

ONE THAN THIS, THAN

TO LAY DOWN ONE'S

LIFE FOR HIS FRIENDS.

JOHN 15:13

What we're really called to do in friendship is to be there for one another. To be there when others have lost their way or have been blown off the trail by the pain of life, by being disillusioned. That's the kind of friend I've tried to be: a "two a.m. friend." The kind of friend someone can call at any time of the day. And even if I don't have the answers, I want to be a friend who says, "Look, I know you're going through some hard stuff, and I may not know the answers to your problems, but I'll sit here with you. I'll give you my shoulder to lean on, and I'll carry you to Jesus."

One of my favorite stories in the Bible is of Jesus healing the paralytic in Mark, chapter two. Four men are friends with a sick man, and they decide they're going to take their buddy to Jesus. Once they make that resolve, nothing can stop them. They probably said, "This is our friend, we care about him, and we're going to get him to Jesus, even if we have to come in through the roof." And that's just what they did. I think that's a great story of what friendship needs to look like.

Throughout the Scriptures, we are constantly urged to have friends within the body of Christ, to be connected to each other, to help each other along the adventure of life. And we need each other. Like the lone antelope trailing from the

group that gets pulled down by the lioness, Satan finds the lone heart a much easier prey than the person who is interconnected with faithful friends.

So we need friends and we need to be a friend, to reach out to others in need. The key element in friendship is service. As chapter fifteen of the Book of John tells us, there is no greater love than self-sacrifice. This is what Jesus demonstrated to His followers time after time. From washing His disciples' feet to the final generosity of the cross, Christ constantly exhibited a life of service.

The greatest person in the kingdom of God is the greatest servant, the greatest friend. So reach out and be a friend. At the same time, don't forget to open your heart and let others reach out the hand of friendship to you. When you're a friend to others, you show them God's friendship with you.

I will be the one you can cry your songs to

My eyes will share your tears

And I'll be your friend if you win

Or if you're defeated

Whenever you need me I will be here

"WHEN YOU ARE A SOLDIER"

From the Sparrow Records release *For the Sake of the Call*

Priorities

BUT SEEK THE KINGDOM OF GOD,

AND ALL THESE THINGS SHALL BE ADDED TO YOU.

LUKE 12:31

here you place your priorities tells the story of your heart. Matthew 6:19–21 says, "Do not lay up for yourselves treasures on earth, where moth and rust destroy and where thieves break in and steal, but lay up for yourselves treasures in heaven. . . . For where your treasure is, there your heart will be also." These verses state this simple truth: what we hold close to our hearts will be the treasure of our hearts. If our hearts hold on to earthly treasures, then those will be reflected in our priorities. But if we hold on to eternal treasures—relationships with people, serving others, serving God and maintaining a personal relationship with Him—then we will have eternal priorities.

We are living in a culture that bombards us with *choices.* We can pick from dozens of kinds of cereals or thousands of CDs! And what about those buffet restaurants? Went I first go into one, I say, "Wow, look at all this great food to choose from!" I then say to myself, "Now, if I get that, I won't be able to eat that, but if I eat more of that, I won't have room for desert." Before long, I'm worn out from making all the choices and wish I could go someplace with just three choices!

With all the choices we have to make in every area of life, how do we choose the best? How do we even distinguish the bad from the good? I wrote "Land of Opportunity" because my desire was to live simply. I find that when you live simply, you purposely eliminate about 85 percent of the choices that are out there.

But how do we decide what are the right priorities? The eternal priorities? God knows what our priorities need to be far better than we do. After all, our perspective is skewed by the bombardment of commercials that tell us, "If you just use this ketchup, your life will be better." God's Word lets us know what our priorities should be, and it's certainly not about more clutter for our lives or more things or more appointments or more money.

My priorities are based on God's Word. First and foremost, I focus on my relationship with God. More than simply a "first" priority, this is the *foundation* for all my priorities. When I love God and serve Him, all the other choices seem to fall into place. I want to love my family well. I want to be a father and a husband who nurtures his family, listens to them, hears the longings of their hearts, and is intimately involved with what is going on in their lives. Beyond that I want to love others, and be aware of their needs. I want to live my life "others-centered."

Even as I say what my priorities are, my conscience reminds me that some days are better than others in sticking to them. But I keep working at it. And that's what the daily adventure of life is all about. Each day is another opportunity to make God our highest priority, to do everything we do for His glory. So if you're a student, do your schoolwork for the glory of God. If you're a mom, love your kids for the glory of God—even wiping noses and changing diapers. If you're a brain surgeon, do it (carefully!) for the glory of God.

This is a world full of options

It's like a never-ending buffet line

While all that I'm really needing

Is living water and the bread of life

"LAND OF OPPORTUNITY"

From the Sparrow Records release *Signs of Life*

Contentment

NOW GODLINESS WITH

CONTENTMENT IS GREAT GAIN.

1 TIMOTHY 6:6

A couple of years ago, I decided to take my family with me to some concerts in South Africa. It was a relatively quiet year for my career; I had taken a sabbatical from most of my singing responsibilities. But it was also a turbulent, worrisome year—shootings took place at my old high school in Paducah, Kentucky, and our close friend, little Erin Mullican, died in a tragic car accident.

I was really looking forward to this trip to South Africa. I planned to do a few concerts, but mostly it was going to be a time for our family to be together and enjoy each other. We were going to do some mission work together and visit other mission works that we were supporting.

As we boarded the flight, I was totally upbeat and excited. I was prepared for a great time. What I wasn't prepared for was an arduous sixteen-hour flight—especially when Caleb spilled his third Sprite. It was running down his leg and my leg. Everything was gooey; we were literally sticking to each other. I had wanted a family bonding experience, but not like this!

About that time, I started feeling restless and very discontent. As I sat there I talked to God about the situation. "Father, why am I so restless? So unhappy? I thought this trip would be a great thing. I thought I was doing something really good, something for You. Why am I so dissatisfied?"

God began to show me that contentment is not determined by location or circumstances. It's determined by the attitude of the heart in that location or circumstance. I remembered Psalm 46:10, "Be still and know that I am God." I felt God saying that the way for me to find contentment was to rest and be still in the knowledge that He was in control . . . of everything. Even the spilt Sprite that was making my pants stick to my leg!

This was an important truth for me to learn. By nature I'm a noisy person. When I'm in the car, I reach for the radio. I'm uncomfortable sitting in the quiet. But when we're still and quiet, we take away all the distractions. Then all of a sudden, it's just us and our hearts and God, and that can be a frightening place. That's where we realize we're not God; we're not in control. We realize how small and tiny we are in comparison to all that is around us. And that is when we experience contentment, how we can accept whatever God brings our way each day. We know that He knows what's going on, and that's enough.

Be still and know that He is God
Be still and know that He is holy
Be still oh restless soul of mine
Bow before the prince of Peace
Let the noise and clamor cease
Be still and know that He is God

"BE STILL AND KNOW"

From the Sparrow Records release *Speechless*

THE *Journey* OF *Life*

. . . FOR I HAVE LEARNED IN

WHATEVER STATE I AM, TO BE CONTENT.

PHILIPPIANS 4:11

he journey you're embarking on will be different than you think. Any adventure you undertake—whether it's schooling, a new job, moving to a new home, or something else—won't be as you imagined it. As I can vouch from personal experience, marriage will be more difficult than you can imagine, and so much more rewarding than you can dream.

Oswald Chambers says, "What we call the process, God calls the end." The journey itself, the process itself, is God's purpose for us. We live in such a goal-oriented society today. Everything is about reaching that final destination, about reaching graduation and then about reaching retirement. We can work and work and work and miss out on enjoying the process of the journey itself. There's a joy to the journey, not just in the high points, but in the hardships too.

Yes, we're traveling toward the end of the journey, but the process of walking that path is the point of the journey. It's a bit like this great trip we took our kids on a few years ago. We decided the whole family would travel together out West. We wanted to see Yosemite and Yellowstone National Parks and the Grand Canyon. We made a big loop and spent about three weeks traveling to each of our destinations.

We saw the Grand Canyon and went to San Francisco to see a baseball game. We also went to Yellowstone and saw Old Faithful. While those phenomenal attractions were definitely part of what made it a great trip, the truly memorable times were the experiences we shared together in the little stops along the way—the little restaurants, the little stores. It was the time we spent with each other during the trip that actually made the trip worthwhile.

I've also learned a lot about the importance of the journey from my good friend and writing collaborator on many of my songs, Geoff Moore. He's introduced me to a world of adventurous activities, from snorkeling to scuba diving to riding motorcycles. In fact, every year we ride the Natchez Trace National Scenic Trail together on our motorcycles.

I tend to be a goal-oriented person, so at the start of each day on the Trace, my first question is, "Okay, where are we going today?" Or I'll make a specific suggestion for the day: "Okay, today I want to get to the Loveless Café where those delicious biscuits and country ham are waiting for me. Let's get going!" I operate that way. I want to get to the place where I want to get to . . . *now*. But Geoff patiently reminds me that we don't take the trip just to get to Natchez, Mississippi, but to enjoy the journey along the way—the little stops, the great food, and the companionship.

I'm the first to admit that learning to enjoy the journey itself has been a challenge. I've written songs like "Not Home Yet" and even an instrumental on the album *Speechless* called "The Journey" to try to overcome my habit of always wanting to get going on the journey. But more and more, I think God is patiently teaching me the importance of the joy of the journey. He's helping me to slow down and savor the small things that happen along the way. He keeps reminding me that the process *is* the journey.